MENAC

another animal alphabet

Poems by Richard Bonfield

COYPU PUBLICATIONS

COPYRIGHT

First published in 2004 by
Coypu Publications,
The Maltings
18 Poppy Close
Leicester
LE2 6UR

with the help of The Zookeepers

ISBN 09521016 2 9

Printed by Modern Press
Santaren Road, Tharston, Long Stratton, Norfolk NR15 2NZ
On re-cycled paper.

FOREWORD

A decade has passed since the publication of "A Bestiary" my first animal alphabet in 1993 and during this period I find that I have once again amassed a Menagerie of creatures both real and imagined, so much so that I have felt the need to increase the size of my original ark in order to accommodate them, hence the publication of this new volume.

This particular Menagerie is a zoology of my peculiar imagination. Others have created real Menageries to satisfy their particular curiosities concerning the animal world and these range from the beasts brought together to provide public pleasure at the Coliseum to the private assemblages of kings and potentates.

There was once a Menagerie at the Tower of London, replete with tigers and lions, and Victorian London had its own house of wonders where elephants and other fantastical creatures were exhibited for the public gaze.

A more enlightened approach to the custody of animals began with the opening of Regents Park Zoo on April 27th 1828

By one of those strange quirks of fate which seem to surround me, April 27th is my birthday and ever since learning of this fact I have felt even more certain that my destiny is in some way bound up with the fate of the animal kingdom.

Of course the early zoos, although more enlightened than their predecessors, were still primarily cages of curiosity around which those creatures at the "apex" of the evolutionary chain, namely ourselves, could perambulate to gaze at the wonder and diversity of those "lower" on the evolutionary ladder. Animals in zoos are excised from their true ecologies. They are not connected to the natural world of which we all form an interdependent part and in this sense, they are living lessons in how we should NOT interact with the animal kingdom. Nevertheless, given the current planetary crisis zoos have now developed a new and much more enlightened role as oases in which creatures, threatened by humanities unbridled greed and ecological corruption, are offered a chance of possible redemption and they are also places we may go to wonder and ponder on what we stand to lose.

Despite the parlous state of the planet and the fact that we appear as a species to be single-handedly orchestrating the next global extinction, there are cautious grounds for optimism, as people of all ages, races, colours and creeds fight for their rightful inheritance.

There is no doubt that many species have already been lost in this present century and countless thousands of others will also be lost to us that we have never had the chance to catalogue; such is the progligacy of the rain forests and abundance the oceans. However, I for one would be saddened if I could only tell my grand- nephews and nieces about tigers as a bedtime story.

We must somehow achieve sustainability and ecological balance for the sake both of ourselves and the wider world, of which we are just one link, albeit self - conscious self -critical and therefore ultimately supremely accountable for the rest of the great chain of being.

Animals allow us to reflect on ourselves. We use them as a mirror, through which to view our various noble and ignoble aspects, but we must never forget that they exist as mystical entities in their own right and that they are inextricably bound up with ALL our ultimate destinies.

" Touch a flower and you trouble a star."

Thankfully the animals, both mythical (on this astral plane at least) and material in my Menagerie, are only caged by the bars of my imagination which is porous and permeable.They are free to come and go as they please.

Some poems here are designed to make you laugh, some to make you ponder, some to make you weep and some to simply make you wonder. Some use animals to allow us to reflect on ourselves, but others allow us just to marvel at life's abundant mystery.

If we go far enough back in time we are all one and we do not cease to be one because of today's apparent diversity.

Let us hope that we never lose that sense of wonder. It's up to all of us. The World is in our hands.

As I said in my last introduction a decade ago, "We're all Noah now."

Richard Bonfield, The Maltings, Leicester April 2004

P.S All is not lost...! YOU too can make a difference. Simply turn to the information on The British Trust for Conservation volunteers at the back of the collection and see how you can get involved. There's a BTCV branch on YOUR doorstep. So, whether you fancy dry stone walling in The Lake District, globetrotting to save the leatherback turtles off the coast of Panama or working to improve bio-diversity in Lord of the Rings Country via one of BTCV's many outreach programmes involving other conservation bodies around the world, assisting the campaign to save the water vole in Yorkshire or simply helping the friendly chain gang in your local neck of the woods, all you have to do is call.

Whatever you do, you're bound to meet some kindred spirits, learn practical conservation skills, help save the planet and have a great deal of fun at one and the same time - and you can't say that of many organizations. So go on... get those green wellies on, pop down to your local branch and be prepared to get down and dirty.

You know it makes ecological sense....!

ACKNOWLEDGEMENTS

My thanks go to the respective editors of the magazines in which
many of these poems first appeared (or are soon to appear)

BBC Wildlife Magazine, Candelabrum, Exile, First Time, The Haiku Quarterly, Iota, Krax, Moonstone, Pagan Dawn, Peer Poetry,
Pennine Ink, Pennine Platform, Pentacle,
Poetry Monthly, Poetry Nottingham International, Reach, Triumph Herald, Still,
Still on Line and TVP.

The poems Horse Whisperer, Kangaroos, Night Thoughts of an Oak Tree and Factory Farmed were
First Prize Winners in The Reach Poetry Competition

Turin Shroud was chosen as one of the top 100 poems by
The Forward Press in 2000.

Zooplankton was a prize winner in The BBC Wildlife Magazine
Poet of the Year Competition in 2002

The illustrations in this collection were taken from:
Knight's Pictorial Museum of Animated Nature
Knight's Pictorial History of England in Two Volumes
Life and her Children by Arabella Buckley
Winner's in Life's Race by Arabella Buckley
Animated Nature by Oliver Goldsmith
The Water Babies by Charles Kingsley
The Scripture Picturebook

Posthumous thanks to their respective illustrators

Listed below are all those who contributed either fiscally, skill wise and or both to the
Genesis of the present collection:

Without them Ark 2 would never have left dry dock, so thanks a million to all concerned.

Dorothy Aitken, Jean and Paul Amphlett, Richard Austin and Family, Art Bailey and Family, Dot and Paul Baker, Jade Blackistone,
Joan Bonfield, Beryl and Vic Bonfield, Bernard O'Brien (Not forgetting "My Friend Arthur"!), Margaret Bultitude and Family, Sara
Clark, Martin Cook, Janine Crowcombe and family, Dr M Davies and family, Diane and Peter Eaton, Barbara Ellis, Lucy Ellis, Edwin
and Pam Faulkner, Wendy Gaston, David and Family, Caroline Gill, Audrey Goaley, Steve and Yvonne Goaley and Family, Patrick
Goodall and Family, David and Greta Groves, John and Shirley Gough, Jim Gray, Leslie Haisman, Gerald and Sheila Hampshire, Denise
Margaret Hargrave, Judith Havens, Christine Hewson, Annie Holgate, David Holliday, Martin Holroyd, Wendy Hooke, Eileen Hubbard,
Barry James, Peter Jarvis, Jayadeva, Jayne Johns, Jade and Veryan Kennedy, Mary and Roy McClean, Marjory Millwood, Helen Mitchell,
Minka Nicholson and Family, James Pearson, Liz Pearson, Claire Piggott, Mike Riddle, Jean and Pat o'Rourke, Pam Russell, David and
Ursula Sainsbury, Alan Scrase, Shantiq, Andrea Slater, Toni Syret, Alison Towndrow, Shirley Turner, Grace Watson, Eric and Marie
Wright, Ian Wright.
And last, but by no means least...! Linda, Jim and Emma, Mike and Treece.

Many thanks to Helen Mitchell and all at BTCV for allowing themselves to be press-ganged as my charity of choice. Information
about their activities and how you can help to conserve our environmental heritage on the priciple
"Think Global Act Local" can be found at the back of the collection.

DRAMATIS PERSONAE

Richard Bonfield - Poems and overall concept

Martin Cook - Page layout, cover design and inside cover photomontages

Art Bailey - Animal alphabet calligraphy

Judith Havens - Proof reading

Patrick Goodall - Inside front and back cover photo

CONTENTS

And nature, the old Nurse, took
The child upon her knee,
Saying "Here is a story book
Thy Father hath written for thee.

"Come wander with me," she said,
"Into regions yet untrod,
And read what is still unread
In the manuscripts of God."

And he wandered away and away
With Nature, the dear old Nurse,
Who sang to him night and day
The rhymes of the universe.

Longfellow

"All living creatures are, so to speak, sparks from the radiation of
God's brilliance, and these sparks emerge from
God like the rays of the sun."

Hildegard of Bingen: The Book of Divine Works

For the late Ted Hughes
and my mother and father
In appreciation.

"He prayeth well who loveth well
Both man and bird and beast;
He prayeth best who loveth best
All things both great and small:
For the dear God who loveth us,
He made and loveth all."

Coleridge

NUMINOUS NATURE

Within the spark
Of other eyes
The mark of The Creator lies

In birds that fly
In fish that swim
The numinous are on the wing

In trees that fruit
And stars that fall
Design is written on the wall

In things that walk
And climb and crawl
Effulgent light envelops all

And all of life's creation floats
Embroiders crucifixion's cloak

But we as humans fail to see
The lights around Golgotha's tree
For we most numinous of all
Were made self-conscious by the fall
And stumble blindly on the ground
Whilst Paradise lies all around.

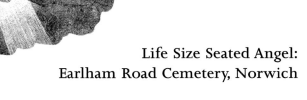

Life Size Seated Angel:
Earlham Road Cemetery, Norwich

An angel sits upon a grave
Her sculpted wings are slightly raised
And if you look into her eyes
The sorrow of the world's implied

She's waiting for our worlds to end
And every grave has such a friend

Wild leaves reach out around her head
Like something almost being said
They weave a wreath round every ledge
A halo for the dancing dead

If lips could speak so carved in stone
She'd tell us we are not alone
We all have angels by our beds
They sit with us from birth to death
And if we ask they'll take our hands
And lead us to the promised land
And if we don't they'll still be there
To comfort us in our despair

I see this angel every week
But of my own I cannot speak
I only know that she is there
And runs her fingers through my hair

An angel sits upon a grave
Her sculpted wings are slightly raised
And as I gaze into her eyes
The wings of Isis open wide.

Wandering Albatross

The loneliest of all the birds
That glides across our lonely world

A solitary curve of white
That soars across the empty night

Across the icebergs far away
The snowflake pilgrim makes his way

Then shipwrecks in a sunbeam's ray
Dissolves into the light of day.

Ant Eater

Of fly-paper his tongue is made
Of platinum his clawing spades
Cyclonic is his swinging nose
This Dyson of the termite groves.

Argonaut: For Kahil Gibran

Floating in the heartlit flood
In the ovoid loom of the womb
Love is weaving an ark of life
A coracle of tiny bones
A vestige from an ancient sea
A brilliant scrap of destiny
Entwined around a fleur-de-lys
A brain that's made of flowers and light
A spine that's carved from anthracite
A ribcage that contains the air
A skull that's fleeced with seaweed hair
And through those eyes the doors of time
A creature looks not yours not mine
But something other shuffling through
A Moses in a caul of blue
A sailor made with gentle glue
A stowaway that time re-drew
Keelhauled upon the wheel of strife
Another being crying "life"
Press-ganged to join the Gaian crew
This argonaut from me to you.

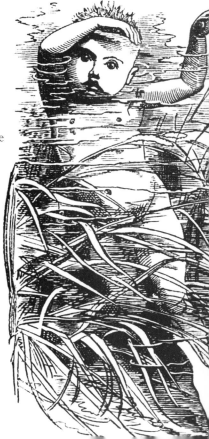

Horse Whisperer:
For G.K. Chesterton

I was the ass that bucked and brayed
Before the crowds that wept and prayed

Upon my back a gentle man
Reached out his gently loving hand

He calmed me with a whispered kiss
I never knew a man like this

The palm fronds gently paved our way
Before he left he gave me hay

And said he'd come to whisper signs
To tame all men ..and make them kind

Then said he'd been...in Herod's time
A stable boy from Palestine.

B

Badger

Painted with strokes of moonlight
The badger shuffles from the dark

Like a part of the dark advancing

The night-sky
Caught in ambling time-lapse

Stars spark from his town-lit eyes
As this confederate of the constellations
This charcoal woodsman
Prowls his monochrome kingdom

Drifting down the path between dusk and dawn

Melting with the morning
Like night fog
Lifting.

Shamanic Dreams

It is as if a glacier has calved
And brought forth the living presence of the land
Or an Inuit child has made a snow bear
From the snowflakes of his thought
Which was absent in the morning
Leaving only tracks in the stillness

Yet somewhere his bear is moving
Loping under the borealis
A lonely thought in the greater loneliness
Somewhere his bear is waiting
Dreaming a white dream

Somewhere his bear is waiting
Dreaming the dreams of a bear
Dreaming the dreams of a child
Dreaming the dreams of them both

Quiet as a cat by a mouse-hole
Dreaming a seal into existence.

hUnny I luv "U"

The eskimos hav 18 difrent names for snow
And today's snow wazn't like any snow I now
But... in the absense of an eskimo
Piglet and I hav decided to call it

"snow" ?

I hav a similar problem with luv

The misstiks hav 18 difrent names for luv
And today's luv waznt like any luv I new
But... in the absence of a wizer pooh
Piglet and I hav decided to call it
"hUnny" with a Kapital "U"!

My Sweet Lord:
For George Harrison (1943-2001)

Here comes the sun
Through winter trees
A sitar on the evening breeze

So let it be
All things must pass
And gently weep
Through leaves of grass

Here comes the sun
Through winter trees
A sitar on the evening breeze

So let it be
All things must pass
But love remains

And love will last.

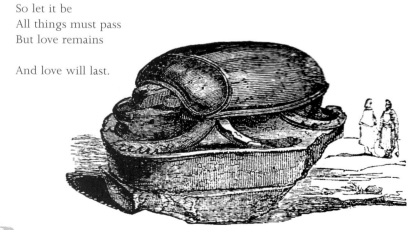

B

Dodgson's Bumble Bee: Bumble Bee Through the Looking-Glass

If summer has a thrumming note
It issues from a bumble's throat
All tiger-striped and furry-skinned
A mustard pot with clockwork wings.

For Mary Webb

The first bee
Milks the last snowdrop
Of winter honey.

Open all Flowers

The bee has been drinking in various flowers
At the height of the summer they're open all hours
But mixing your nectars is not very wise
And can lead to problems returning to hives.

In the honeycomb of my head
Poems are distilled
From the wild flowers of adventure.

Sutton Hoo Helmet

Who gazed through these moonless eyes
And lay within this ghostly ship?
For thirteen hundred acid years
The thief of time devoured his gifts
Yet even time could not dissolve
The timeless glint of timeless gold
The bird that framed these moonless eyes
That gazed out over storm-lit skies
His soul flew briefly through the hall
Then arced through windows dark and tall
He flew into the Pagan night
Or did he find the light of Christ?
He lies between these drifting lands
A shifting soul on shifting sands
A Janus looking back and forth
From Christian South to Viking North
To Valhalla or Avalon
To which one has the storm cock gone?
A weather-vane upon a hill
His spirit drifts about here still.

Note on Poem. The defining feature of the Sutton Hoo helmet is the gilded bird that delineates
the eyebrows/ wings, nose/body and moustache/tail feathers of the moonless face.
The owner of the helmet is thought on good authority from a variety of sources to be Raedwald
one of a line of Saxon Kings who ruled East Anglia at this time.

The complex of Sutton Hoo is seen by many as a pagan redoubt surrounded by a Christian sea,
but the tide was turning and certain Kings in Sweden who were buried in ship mounds were later
re-interred by their recently converted sons in newly built churches hard by the promontories of
the old religion.

The Sutton Hoo helmet is associated in the popular imagination with BEOWULF the hero figure of
the poem of the same name which lies like a great Viking burial mound filled with a glittering
word hoard at the very beginnings of English literature.

The poem was written sometime in the eighth century (around the time that the complex of
Sutton Hoo was being created) by an anonymous Christian monk and, although the poem harks
back to an earlier period in Scandinavian history, there were strong links between the Danish and
Anglo Saxon cultures and for many the Sutton Hoo helmet IS the helmet of the mythic hero who
defeated Grendel.

Bittern

Once Bittern
Twice shy.......

Blackbirds

The flautist with the golden beak
Who lulls you off to lovely sleep
Is singing in a nearby tree
And when you're tucked up safe and sound
His melody drifts all around
A song that pours from summer earth
Like pennies from a velvet purse
As all around our sunset town
The blackbirds bring the curtain down.

Beside the old lock
This scented buddleia
Bright with summer pilgrims.

Bob Hope's Camel

Martian hooves
A hairy hump
A wild odiferous
Fly whisked rump

The Ancient World is her spittoon
Her breath would make an old skunk swoon

Her teeth were nicked from King Tut's mother
Her lips are made of Indiarubber

Her song is like the muezzin's call
As from the minaret he falls

Her manners are uncouth and slow
Her legs are knock-kneed down below

And yet her eyes are liquid gold
The desert's pouting centrefold

And in a mirage she may seem
Like Debbie Reynolds in a dream
To dance around your caravan
Whilst on the road to Samarkand.

Epiphany

A cold coming he had of it
The camel bearing Balthasar
Across the desert's frosted fields
Under the light of the Bible's star
But warmth he found in nuzzled straw
Upon The King of Heaven's floor.

Sam Gamgees's Carp

His scales are tiles from elven halls
The leaves of mallorn in the fall
His coat of mithril's finely wrought
Embossed with gold from Gondor's court
The sunfish of freshwater streams
The evening's last refulgent gleam
He slips behind the misty peaks
Of Minas Tirith wreathed in sleep.

Evening Carp

We sat at the head of the lake
And watched the great carp roll
In the lengthening evening
Splashing in the sunset of our glasses.

Glastonbury Carp

Older than the pool is old
Solder laced with scales of gold
Covered in the verdigris
Accrued throughout the centuries
The carp lies many fathoms deep
A sunset caught in carved relief
The wisest thing within the mere
The breastplate laid on Arthur's bier.

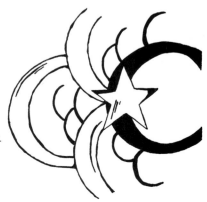

For Paddy (1984-1998)

After 14 years
The cat-flap still
The autumn moon on the empty garden.

Children of Albion

An ox an ass
A manger
Straw

Well this is what the children draw

And on The Lake of Galilee
Potato prints splosh out at sea

And on a hill there's Postman Pat
Who's watching Jesus with his cat

And on a cross a gold-topped man
Is crucified by Pritt-Stick hands

If we could draw what children draw
Then we would see what Jesus saw

But growing old we rub away
The crayoned star from Christmas Day.

Gethsemane Cockerel

I was the cock
Who crowed at two
When Peter said
"I know not you"

I was the cock
Who crowed at three
When Peter said
"I am not me"

I was the cock
Who crowed no more
When Peter wept
And truly saw

I was the cock
At Heaven's door
When God went
To the threshing floor.

Celtic Cockerel: Buttermere

A letter from The Book of Kells
Illuminates the frosted fells
And celebrates The Book of Life
A page turned on a winter's night.

Dream of the Cormorant Fisherman

In the night sky
My cormorant dives
Amongst shoals of stars.

Crayfish

Little lobster of my dream
Rowan-berried eggs unseen
Lift her up and see them gleam
Hedge-roes in a mountain stream.

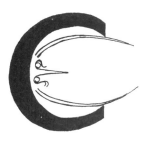

Curlews

Northumbrian pipes
In moorland air

Wild wheeling sadness
Everywhere.

Curlews

Above the sunrise curlews swirl
Through thyme and space their cries unfurl
Until they dip beneath the world
To nest on moons of speckled pearl.

Fallow Deer

They move like light through summer trees
Attended by a limpid breeze

They ripple like a moving wave
Like flames inside a coral cave

They flow like water over glass
Like players in a summer masque

And then their evening shadows pass
Like velvet over Glyndebourne grass.

Deer in Earlham Road Cemetery Norwich..?

It was Bruce who told me there were
Deer in the cemetery

Hidden under small trees
Blooming at dusk

Somehow they had seeped through railings
Painted themselves in with a velvety brush

To leave on the air
in the dew of the morning

A faint efflorescence
Like sweet spirits laughing

The scent of their passing

The lawns tinged with musk.

Roe Deer

Amongst the forest saplings moved
Small dappled trees with cloven hooves

They shifted in the changing light
Their gilded haunches poised for flight

And then they washed across the glade
And as they dried began to fade

Their forms receding up the glen
And melting round the twilight ben.

Guide Dog

A man's golden eyes
Doors of perception
On all fours
Love in harness
The labrador leads her master
Through invisible cities

She waits
With the patience of Job
By rush hour roads
Leads her master
Through the red sea of impatient steel

Curled at his heel
She is his sign and seal

A symbiosis through patient osmosis
The Ariadne who guides him through
The sound filled tunnels of a sunless world.

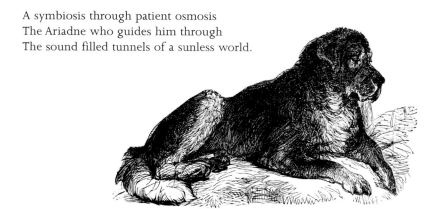

Sheepdog

A four-legged field radio
A scampering chessboard
Alert to every whistling nuance
The sheep-shadower
Slouches and sleuths
On invisible strings of obedience
Dancing to the skylark of a man's fluted fingers
And the sheep are nudged by waves of fear
Bolstering together
In exact increments of terror
As the sheepdog quivers at the edge of instinct
Balanced on the razor between hunt and herd
Poised at the still point of the rustling heather.

Dormouse Dreaming

Curled up
Like a pocket watch
The dormouse ticks
The dormouse tocks
Until her paws say
Five-to-spring
For then the clock's
Alarm bell rings
And from a waistcoat's downy pocket
The March hare opens
Winter's locket
To tell the dormouse that it's time
To wake up from this yawning rhyme.

Dormouse Triptych

The dormouse
Has made her winter billet
In the shape of the earth
Tucked her claws
Into the gloves of her ears

Turned her heart down
To a careless whisper

Outside the snow falls
In white epiphanies
And the cold sears all things
But the dormouse does not know
What winter brings

A creature of three seasons
She blossoms with the flowers
Scurries through eternal summer
Tiptoes into weeping autumn

Climbs into the teapot of her harvest home
Dreams under the night-light of the North Star.

Dragonfly

A flying boat
Of weightless glass
The stained glass insect
Makes a pass
And tilts upon her fragile pins
To catch the summer on her wings.

Autumn Dragonfly

A lovely flying Celtic cross
Her fuselage of dreams embossed
With stained glass windows
Dipped in frost.

Sunset Dragonfly

Here he comes
Whirling from the prehistoric
Graduating from the soup kitchens
Of summer streams
With his honeycomb goggles
And his soap bubble wings
Da Vinci's swirling rotor blades
Emerging from the autumn haze
An ash seed spinning in the dusk
A bow tie flecked with wanderlust.

A Klondyke of gold-rush wings
Pans the hare
From a bowl of hills.

Golden Eagle

A golden beak
An upswept feather
A lectern
Tossed in stormy weather
Across the Highland's purple heather
There floats a laird
In search of treasure

His fiefdom is the northern sky
The midnight sun enrobes his eye

And as he eddies through the fog
His subjects sense the wrath of God

A ringwraith sweeping up Glen Coe
His claymores raking bounding snow.

Exposition of The Elephant Man:
For John Merrick,
A cultured and graceful human being

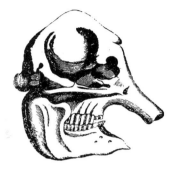

"Lay your sleeping head my love
The world
Was never good enough."

Examine here in grotesque form
This aberration from the norm
The bulbous head
Beneath this sack
The "lithsp" with which it answers back
This monster shows how far we've risen
From lesser creatures in their prisons
This beast is something caught between
The missing link that haunts our dreams
We should be thankful as we gaze
That we have risen from the caves
To stand as Lords of all Creation
And pity those of lower station
Who cannot think or feel as we
Encased in brute biology.

Barbara Cartland's Flamingo

The flamingo is so very pink
She blushes when she stoops to drink

She's Barbara Cartland's favourite bird
That mistress of the rosebud word

And when she flies into the sun
The colours of her wing tips run

To paint a soft carnation dusk
That's filled with sugar-coated lust.

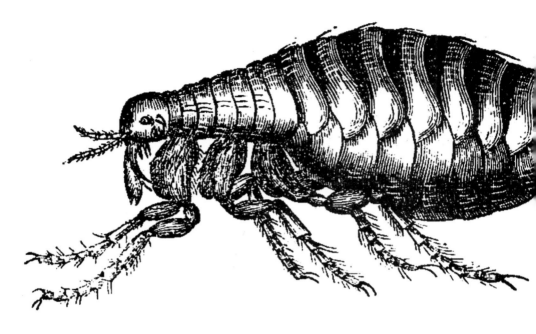

Flea

If you could leap The Empire State
Or windsurf on a Martian Sea
You would achieve
In human terms
The prowess of the tiny flea
Who takes such measures in his stride
Whilst abseiling an Elk Hound's side
Or climbing up a Polar Bear
An Everest of frosted hair.

F

A Poem for Flidais:
Irish Goddess of the Woods

I am the Goddess of the woods
A spirit seldom understood

Great Herne the hunter is my groom
He rules the sun I rule the moon

And when the sun shines on the land
He takes me by my milk-white hand

And leads me up the woodland path
To make green love upon the grass

And when the waves break on the sand
He gives to me a Celtic band

A ring that's made of emerald stones
He found within a hill of bones

And when the snow lies on the path
We gather round the sacred hearth

To pluck love from the dulcet harp
And bless The New Year's pulsing heart.

Thoughts on the 'Thought Fox' by Ted Hughes

The fox has left the bookshop shelves
The trap's been sprung by we ourselves
For art is under lock and key
But all can shoplift poetry
So everyone who feels emotion
Can keep the Thought Fox as a totem
He lives inside as many heads
As scan the snow he softly treads
This poem may be a national treasure
But everyone can poach its pleasure
The fox is there for all to find
He waits to enter every mind
Created out of ink and paper
His world is there for every taker
And therein lies the wealth of words
More priceless than a poacher's birds
That midnight moment on the page
Which will endure from age to age
Wherever those who read or write
Can scan the forests of the night
And watch The Thought Fox boldly come
When snow and ink and brain are one.

Urban Fox

There she goes
The urban fox
With moonlight spittle
On her chops

Our bags been burgled
In the night

By something red
And sharp and bright

The country's running through the town
A vixen on the Underground.

Fox in the Night

The russet stink
Of brushwood red
A gosling taken
From its bed
The farmer standing
On the lawn
A barn door
Swinging in the storm.

Winter Fox

The fox's brush paints his winter shadow
As he dips his tuft in aniseed moonlight
And leaves his scent for the trailing hounds
Who have stink-visions dreaming in their baying beds
Of steaming innards, dismembered legs
Who can smell the prey in his reeking hose
As he leads them on by the frosted nose
There's a smell consensus in their pell-mell pursuit
As they shadow the quarry with his aromatic loot
Until they lose him by a double-crossing coombe
As the fox swims over a howling moon.

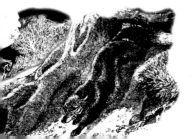

Gannets at Sunset

They dive
Like Acapulco men
Beneath the waves
And up again
They learn to plunge
In silent streams
A flock of falling guillotines
White Stukas of the ocean air
They dive-bomb with unerring flair
A rain of arrows from the fold
To strafe the oceans cloth of gold
Returning to the evening sky
With gobbets of stargazey pie
Wild pirates of the azure foam
All Neptune's archers flying home.

Gecko

A delicate lizard
With fly paper feet
The Gecko can squirm
Over ceilings or seats

For the heavens are just as safe
As a chair

When you're light as a feather
And 'velcroed' to air.

Call of the Wild

The vastness of the harvest sky

The greylags elegiac sky
Across the windswept autumn earth
Their instincts urge

Disperse...
Dispe

Transition

Wheeling like escaping leaves
The geese sweep over sleeping trees

Their destination is the sun
That shines beyond the fowler's gun

And as they flicker overhead
The Autumn turns his burning head

To watch the Summer passing by
As comets light the geese filled sky.

Up above the sky is blue
The geese call over fields of dew
And as I watch I think of you
Arm in arm with someone new.

Norfolk-Fly Past

Against the spendour of a Cotman sky
The brush-stroked geese go floating by

And as their skeins bank overhead
The marsh below is flooded red

And as they swing towards the sun
The fowler points his loaded gun

To scatter flocks like hand tossed grain
Dissolving into autumn rain.

The flutes of autumn fly at dawn
When Herne the hunter
Blows his horn.

Christmas Gift

What are the geese pulling
through the frosted air..?

They are pulling the tides
And Autumn's hair

They are coaxing the moon
From her yawning lair

They are sweeping the snow
From the starlit stair

And escaping the jaws of the Polar Bear

What are the geese pulling
Through the frosted air?

They are pulling Winter
On her painted sledge

They are leaving cobwebs
On a frosted hedge

They are sweeping Eastwards
Leaving Springtime's pledge

And a glass of moonlight
On your window ledge.

G

Giraffe

Africa's

    Leaning

        tower

           of

              Pisa.

Giraffes

Have you seen
The leaf eating flowers

The beautiful lolloping
Tangerine towers

Balletic fork-lifts
With cumulus brains

That glimmer across the African plains

To nibble the sunset
Like curious cranes

Then perfume the evening
Like love after rain?

Within the church of my hands
The glow-worms
Harvest candle.

Orion

Look..!
Low in the autumn sky
A glow-worm on the hawthorn.

Winter Goldfish

Under the ice
The goldfish glow
Like Christmas clementines
Wrapped in snow.

G

Goshawk: For T.H. White

A captive cloud leopard
Clasped on the wrist
Like a dark knight that dreams
In the shield feathered lists
This slip streamed crossbow
Of snow sprinkled elms
Twists and burns
In his moon blinkered helm

Then

Flowers above this sun leavened kingdom
To hammer the quarry
In his blood sprinkled realm

Returning again
Like a faithful retainer
Spiralling down to the grain quilted floor
To land again on the wrist of the aimer
Who unleashed this dawn dappled

Minion of war.

Grendel

Marsh flaring eyes
Dripping into The Dark Ages
With a six-pack of men.

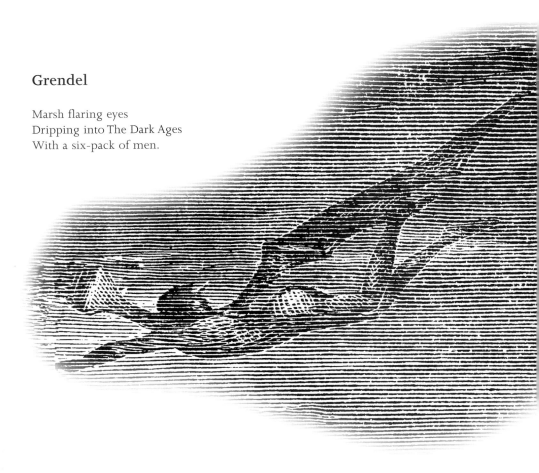

October Night

Last night he came
The Wind Grendel
And took even the little leaves
That slept beneath my Hall of Clouds.

Green Man

I am the voice who sings from trees
My tongues are all unfurling leaves
I am the Greenwood's Lord of mirth
I am the mouthpiece of the earth

I am the Lord of all misrule
I am the singing dancing fool
I am the lych-gate in your soul
That leads you back through fields of gold

I am the seasons passing by
I am the sun who warms the sky
I am the source of all you know
The spring from which all waters flow

I am a clearing in your heart
A quiet place in an antlered park
I am your inner leaf clad guide
I am The Green Man by your side.

Green Spirit of Celtic Place

Wild spirit of this sylvan place
I feel the wind upon my face

I lived here when the world was young
Will live here when the world is gone

And those who come to worship me
Will find me deep within the tree

Will sense me in the hawk that flies
Will catch me on the salmon's tide

For I am born of mystery
Exist outside of history

And give to earth its special grace
The numen filling sacred space

And give to earth its pagan faith
The Goddess with a smiling face.

Crop circle eyes
And clown shoe paws
The southpaw hare
For a Mad March Dare
Goes Morris Dancing
Over the constellations.

Hare

The hare is the quivering high command
Of hare intelligence
Feeling the wind with his Fylingdale whiskers
Turning his hare-brained velvet radar
His whole early-warning system of hare
Into the twitching landscape
Listening
For the thoughts of foxes
The dreams of eagles
Transfixed in a cat's cradle
Of his own cross-eyed uncertainty
A Jack-in-the box
Waiting to leap
To all points of the compass
A paranoid schizophrenic
Sectioned by his own senses
A harp of hare
Mad as March
Shaking on the edge of his daft horizon
Quaking in the shadow of his own reflection.

Heron

I am rod
And I am line
A switchblade knife
That
Given time
Will turn this millpond into wine
For nature carved me from the air
To be the bird that isn't there
Yet through the looking-glass I spy
The apple of my gimlet eye
I slash down from my mist-wrapped hide
The mirror cracks from side to side
I fly between the dusk and dawn
Leave moonlit scales upon the lawn.

Hippo of Troy

Because the hippo lost her brace
A grave-robbed smile adorns her face

She could have been a pageant queen
A cheer-leader for football teams

Instead she drools from carmine lips
The face that sank a thousand ships.

Hippo

A sumo ballerina
Cavorting with her friends
Auditioning for Swan Lake
In African D.M.s

Pygmy Hippo: Regency Park Zoo

Small and black
Enchantingly fat

A bonsai hippo
Going slappity-slap

A pert but perfect submarine
A black-pudding floating
Through a Yorkshireman's dream

The charmingly wobbly
Cheeseburger fawn

A Nubian jelly
On a Regency lawn.

Maps and Dreams: For Hugh Brody

An Inuit is quickly lost
Amongst the cliffs of London
The iconography defeats him
But in the Arctic he has his own postcode for flowers and whales
He knows where the animals come and go
He goes with the floe
Works with the dream-weaver of the polar web
Knows where the snow spider hides the grail of the narwhal
When the rivers are filled with the potlatch of salmon
He does not travel needlessly to the right address
At the wrong time

The streets of ice are always changing
The whale-road of summer is closed in winter

There is a time and a place for every purpose under heaven
A time to sew a time to reap
A time for giving and a time to keep

The map of the Inuit cannot be folded in a pocket
Or kept like a charm in a silver locket
The dreams of the landscape cannot be bought
They are a tapestry of changing lights
A Bestiary of the polar mind
Illuminated by different animals
At different times

The land is bountiful in due season
And everything appears for a different reason

(In the Palantir of the shaman
The caribou can now be seen on the distant shores of thought
Walking the whale-road in their thousands).

Summer Jabberwocks

Beware the plumptious flying thing
The bottom-burping
Wood pigeon.

Gardez l'eau
At five to two
A Glastonbury port-a-loo....!

Beware the flying vestibule
First cousin to the earthbound mule
Who bucks and brays across the sky
And sprays a silage lullaby.

Melting
On the shore
A Salvador Dali chandelier.

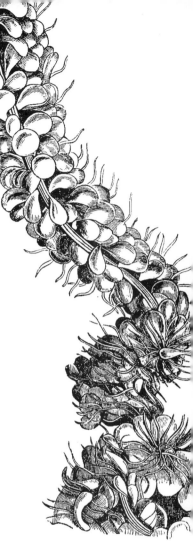

Jellyfish

A pulsar
Winking in the night

A distant fairground's
Fairy lights

The blooms of Neptune
Floating free

The hanging gardens
Of the sea.

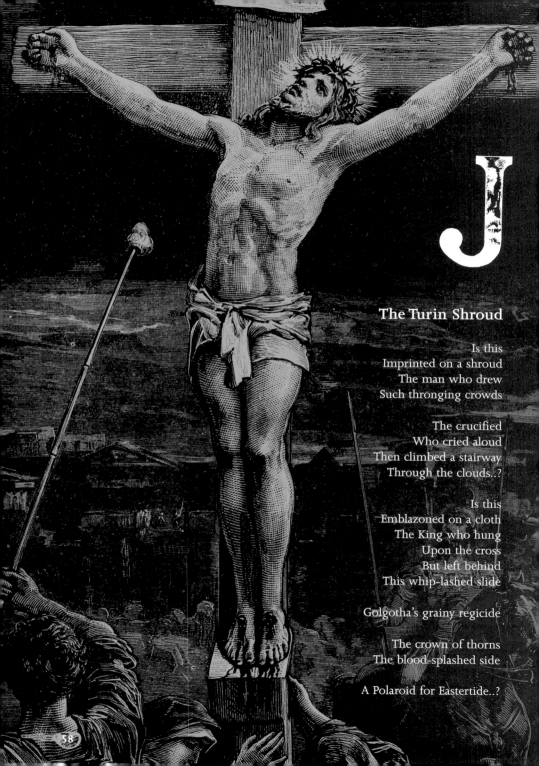

J

The Turin Shroud

Is this
Imprinted on a shroud
The man who drew
Such thronging crowds

The crucified
Who cried aloud
Then climbed a stairway
Through the clouds..?

Is this
Emblazoned on a cloth
The King who hung
Upon the cross
But left behind
This whip-lashed slide

Golgotha's grainy regicide

The crown of thorns
The blood-splashed side

A Polaroid for Eastertide..?

Kangaroos: With Literary Tails

Bouncing across the Nullarbor Plain
Are velvet space-hoppers
With rocking-horse brains

And soft donkey ears
    And bay window wombs
        And fingers like delicate runcible spoons

            Bouncing across the Nullarbor Plain
                Are the rocking-horse chairs
                    In a looking-glass game

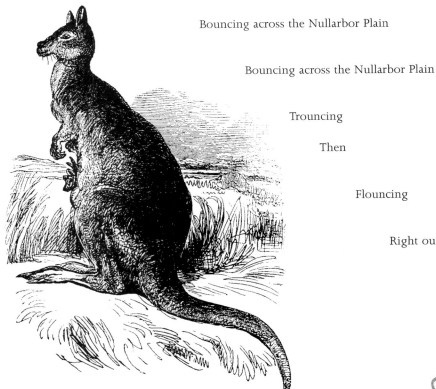

                Bouncing across the Nullarbor Plain

                Bouncing across the Nullarbor Plain

                Trouncing

                Then

                    Flouncing

                        Right out of the frame!

Kingfisher
On the No Fishing sign
...Dripping silver.

September Kingfisher

Trafficlightsblurringinautumnrain.

Think of rainbows in the sky
Then picture this
A bird that flies
With colours pouring from her wings
As in the dusk she sweetly skims
Then twinkles in the evening sun
A jewel thief on the river-run.

Turner's paintbox
Glimpsed in a tangle
Of Winter branches.

Kingfisher's Ring

Bird of the turning earth
Covered in ocean and land
You are the birthstone of Gaia
Worn on her moondancing hand.

Not a Kingfisher: For Magritte

Wrought in all mediums
Metal oil and watercolours
He outflashes them all
Picks all artistic locks
Slip stitches the autumn water
Slips through the finest mesh
Of our finest imaginings
And burns away across an evening river.

Ladybird

Bishy barny bee
Sleeps through snow
Then in the springtime
Ups and goes

A tipsy death-cap
Lipstick sweet
With Buzz-Bee-Berkley
Twinkling feet
That whirrs across the Norfolk skies
A powder puff amongst the flies.

Note on Poem. Bishy barny bee
is Norfolk dialect for ladybird..!

Spring Lambs

Clouds
Born under clouds

Jellied bundles of nimbus
Birth queasy on pipe-cleaning hooves

The first unbalanced fruits of spring
So delicately teetering
Unsteady on the cloven floor
They wobble on the sun swept moor.

L

Lampreys

Freshwater 'slugs'
With watchparts for teeth
Lampreys were served
At large monarch's feasts

But ever since then
Their charm has declined

And no one dines out with lampreys in mind.

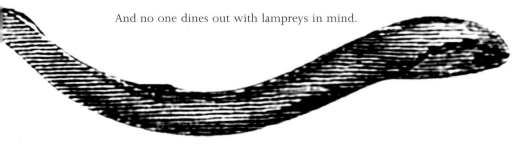

The Legionnaire's Tale:
A lost Chaucerian Fragment

We cast some lots
To take the robe

A roll of dice
For treasure trove

I folded up the caul of God
And with the legions
Miles I trod

I lost it in a tavern brawl
Some gladiator took the shawl

I've searched for it
In many shrines
Purporting to have holy finds

Through many lands
And many times

And then for Turin did I make
To castigate the final fake

Yet when the casque was there undone
I saw the robe that I had won

The very fleece was there unfurled
That cloaked the Saviour of the world

And on it was the thorn scratched face
That welcomed me to Heaven's Gate.

L

Summer has pulled up stumps
And a leveret sleeps
In the batsman's furrow.

Llama 'Kaarma'

I once asked in Lima a llama
What he thought of the doctrine of Karma..?
He replied that he once preached in snow capped Tibet
So poor spelling was something
He'd always regret.

Astrologers

We need them more than they need us
The three kings
Gold leaf blowing in the desert wind

Only in Matthew do they ride across the page
But from these dusty verses
We have tapped an oasis of invention

With their gifts of gold, frankincense and myrrh
They glide on by

For all of us need to be announced
All of us need to be gifted
All of us need to be lifted

All prefigured in some eternal sky.

Magi

Great shadows on a lapis sky
The potentates glide softly by
Encrusted with the emerald earth
They voyage to glimpse a virgin birth

Across the deserts flood of hours
They ply their ships past rose red towers
On palanquins of sumptuous hide
A pearl above their lustrous guide

And every Christmas-time they come
With blazing gifts for Mary's son
Three gilded kings from lands afar

To crown the shepherd of the stars.

Magpies

They're plainly there
In black and white

Their feathers missed
The rainbow's light

But in their nest
A spectrum shines

The jewel-box
Of a concubine.

Magpie

The Magpie
Yearns for the dreamcoat of the Jay

He would love to steal his spectrum away
Be Oscar Wilde
For a year and a day

But black and white are the magpie's lot
He's the transsexual friar
Who dreams of frocks.

Spring in the Arctic

The wind bleached tusk
Of a mammoth
Tinged with golden lichen.

Mammoth Meditation

Siberius standing
For snow swept hours
Lost in a meadow of
Pleistocene flowers.

Mammoth Undertaking

A fork-lift truck
In an Afghan coat

Orson Wells
In an ice cream float

The deepest winter you could dream
The snow plough of the Pleistocene.

Mole

Deep beneath the furrowed land
The blind skin-opener
With his wicket-keeping hands
Is scrabbling through Stygian gloom
Like a venerable scholar
In a starless room
Wading through his Stilton
With a port-stained spoon.

Musk Oxen:
For Barry Lopez

If Jason had sailed North
He would have found The Golden Fleece
Of the Musk Oxen
Ancient cousins of The Grecian Kind

As much a product of this land
As the land itself

The breathing embodiment

As at home here
As we are
Curled up with the Sunday Papers

And he would have marvelled
At their sagacity
Their two million year interrogation
Of the wind
Their made to measure movements
Their diet of fire weed and willow
Darkness and light

And he would have wished
That he too
Could cease his wanderings
Drop anchor in the pack ice
And learn something about patience
Endurance
And the healing to be had
From these hoary Buddhas
Wrapped in snowflakes

Drifting under the Bo Tree of The North Star.

Nautilus

A Danish pastry
In a coral sea

A sauasage curled
In a charcuterie

A whirlpool cupped
In Neptune's hand

The storm-tossed relic
Of a golden ram.

The cartwheel ammonites have gone
The nautilus still lingers on
The Triton horn that Neptune blows
The ocean's lovely floating rose

Okapi

You glimpse her
In the dusky light

The jungle's blushing neophyte
That floats beneath the forest heights
An anagram of striped delights

You glimpse her nibbling
Gliding through

Giraffe and Zebra and Gnu

All blended with a twinkly moo
The shyest geisha in the zoo.

Osprey

My castle is a mountain pine
My window on the west inclines

I am the lord of river bends
The Fisher-King of mountain glens

I am the pendulum that swings
Across the loch with midnight wings

To pluck the salmon from his lie
Haul flapping silver through the sky

The last thing that the salmon sights
The priest who gives the final rites

I glory in my sweeping flights
I plunge across The Northern Lights.

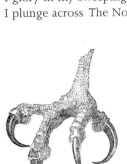

A quizzical ripple
Of twinkling rings
The smile that watches
The North Star
Sing......

Otters

Bright eyed mermammals
Slick backed and sharp suited
Wearing the water like a second skin
Otters disport their barnstorming beauty
Displacing their torsos with web fingered wings
Twisting themselves like gymnasts' ribbons
In arabesques of refracted light
Otters elope through their aqueous kingdom
Like sinuous smoke rings from Poseidon's pipe
Like head-scarves
Cascading from soft-tops in flight
Gawky above but God like below
They glide between worlds like a svelte shadow show
Dissolving in light like a lithe swirling brush
Like the scent of Chanel on a Jaguar's plush
Dissolving in time like a shy geisha's blush
Like a Cheshire Cat's grin
On a loch's midnight hush.

Owl

He hoots beneath the silver moon
His feathers shine
Like gold doubloons

He floats across the evening sky
A dark avenging lullaby.

The Owl's Saga

Tu whit...Tu whoo At Sutton Hoo
A king lies near his motley crew

A silver surfer sleeping proud
Beneath the scudding Suffolk clouds

The white caps of a winter sky
Which broach the mounds where longships lie

And drive a fleet of buried men
To Ragnarok and back again

From there to sail into the west
And reach the mead hall of the blessed.

The Oxymoron

The Oxymoron hunts by night
But sad to say he's not that bright
And sometimes hunts himself by day
And kills himself in the affray.

If a pelican
Why can't a Parma ham..?
Or an Elvis fan..
Or Desperate Dan...?

Cockney Pelicans: Regency Park Zoo

Their beaks are flaccid Gladstone bags
Their belly-cans hold schools of dabs

They congregate like old-time lags
And auction fish for packs of fags.

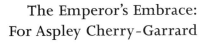

Emperors

Glimpsed through
Winter mists

A swathe of glass-
Blown orchids

A field of starlit
Chessmen

Glazed by the
Midnight sun.

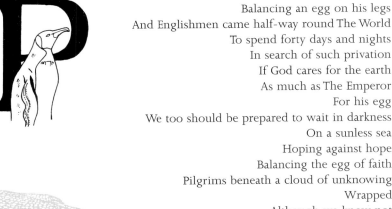

The Emperor's Embrace:
For Aspley Cherry-Garrard

Jesus spent forty days and nights in the Wilderness
Tempted by starvation
And the Devil
The rain lashed the ark
For forty days and nights
This seems the Biblical equivalent
Of the ultimate privation
Yet The Emperor Penguin spends eighty days and nights
In the darkness of the world
Balancing an egg on his legs
And Englishmen came half-way round The World
To spend forty days and nights
In search of such privation
If God cares for the earth
As much as The Emperor
For his egg
We too should be prepared to wait in darkness
On a sunless sea
Hoping against hope
Balancing the egg of faith
Pilgrims beneath a cloud of unknowing
Wrapped
Although we know not
In the wings of God's embrace.

Note on poem. Aspley Cherry-Garrard who wrote the seminal travel book *The Worst Journey in the World* was a member of Scott's expedition who travelled with two companions Bowers and Oates (both of whom who later died in the ill-fated attempt on the Pole) on a winter expedition in search of The Emperor Peguin's eggs. They travelled in some of the most atrocious conditions ever known to man but survived to return with 3 eggs hoping that this hard won prize would increase the sum of human knowledge. In the event the expedition did little to further the sum of human knowledge but much to further spiritual camaraderie in the face of seemingly implacable odds. Somewhere in the heart of that polar darkness there loomed a great and kindly light.

In the corner of a deer-coloured field
This gilded flourish
On a scrap of moonlit vellum.

Pheasant

A first-class bird
In a third-class carriage

For an Asian groom
An unhappy marriage

A Maharajah decked
In silks and pearls

Just cannon-fodder
For Dukes and Earls.

Crowd Pleaser

The pigeon might seem to be a simpleton
But every year he manages to court centre stage
At Lord's Trent Bridge and Wimbledon.

P

Incontinentals

Rent-a-crowd
Mad pigeons
Waddle and warble
Zimmering inanely in the summer square
Posing before particularly imposing bins

You can tell that their brains
Are tiny
Rare perhaps as a Nubian pearl

They are so deliciously stupid
That you wonder if any of them know they are there

Camera-hung you find them
From Basildon to Saint Mark's square
Incontinental tourists
Sans beaks, sans claws, sans brains, sans care.

P

Warm Chorus

We wake to bathe in wood pigeons
A smidgeon of sunlight
Warms our legs.

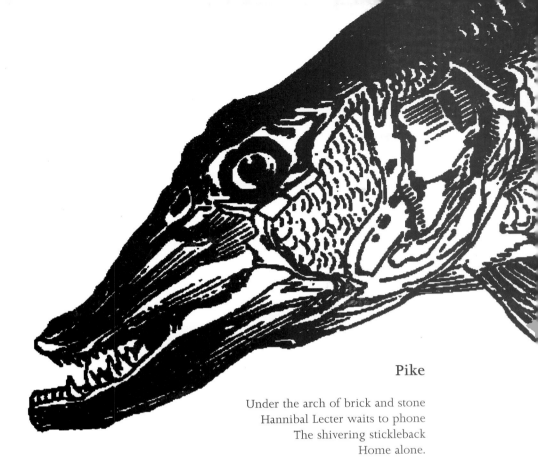

Pike

Under the arch of brick and stone
Hannibal Lecter waits to phone
The shivering stickleback
Home alone.

Platypus Battypus

The platypus is so mixed up
That Freud and Jung both had no luck

They could not cure him come what may
"He's more than the sum of his parts.." they'd say

"We cannot unmix mud from clay.."

"This Antipodean ego is here to stay..!"

And so he remains... in every way
The classic case of Multiple Animal Personality Disorder

To this very day.

Song of Taliesin

I shapeshift into autumn trees
And mourn the waning of their leaves

I glide upon the seventh wave
A salmon leaping to his grave

I as an eagle circle high
Inspect the realms in which I fly

I as a stag ascend the moor
And bellow from a mist-wrapped tor

I as a stone uphold the sky
A menhir till the day I die

I as a shaman enter in
I am the shape of everything.

If poets had to make their own paper
They would take much more care over words
And many would then turn to haiku
Saving more of our timber reserves.

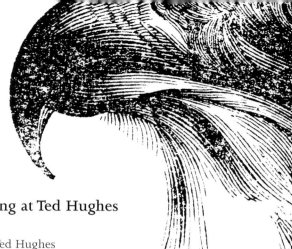

57 Ways of Looking at Ted Hughes

You cannot bottle old Ted Hughes
As Pagan Man
Or Morning Dew

As chutney
Or as Boots Home Brew

For he was morning noon and night
A roe deer on a motor bike

And all of England's Season Songs
Were written with his magic wand

He's like the weather
Always new

The rain the wind the lovely view

And all our green and troubled land
Is found in poems

Hughes has canned.

Epitaph for Ted Hughes

A great oak felled on a windswept moor
A Druid closing summer's door
A salmon beached beneath a tor
The shapeshifter will shape no more.

P

Puffin

A stubby
Windlit Spitfire
A portly angel
Caught between the stools
Of water and sky
A half-way house of an absurd bird
For his flying degree
He scraped a third
King of his Hebridean sand eel castle
Thinks of himself as an air-vice-marshall
Great for pillows and manure
Careening amongst the streamlined skuas
Tasty as duck
Eggs reeking of muck
Full of his own clumsy self-importance
Always takes the same sea-musty chalet
From which to perform his juddery ballet
Electrifying underwater
The wing-tip glider for Neptune's daughter
Has that little islander mentality
A private in charge
Of a principality
Wears his medals from previous wars
Everyone fought for a righteous cause
Winters in more southern climes
Thinks Mateus Rosé a decent wine
Loves his eel pie
Loves his wife
For a wind-blitzed spitfire
It's a puffin's life.

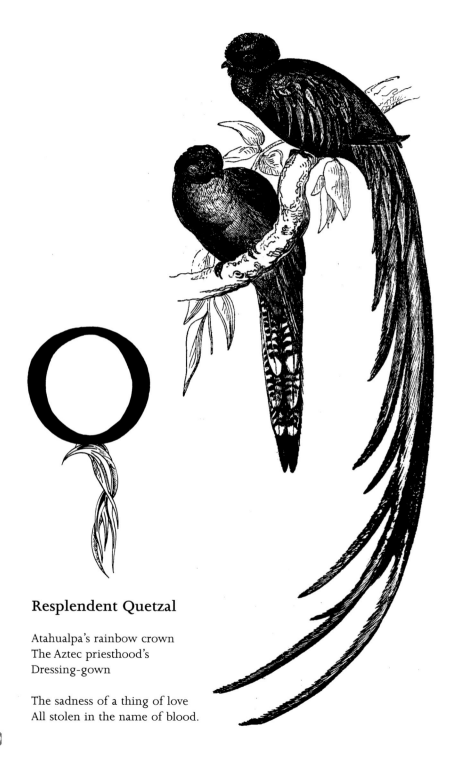

Resplendent Quetzal

Atahualpa's rainbow crown
The Aztec priesthood's
Dressing-gown

The sadness of a thing of love
All stolen in the name of blood.

Rhinoceros

Durer's engraved behemoth
Descendent of Triceratops

He lurches on the dust filled plain
A quivering horn-capped mountain range

A tank with sides of dimpled iron
Impregnable to prides of lions

A fossil from another age
That rumbles down this printed page...

He's Rommel in a leather coat
Binoculars around his throat

He's Goering in an armoured car
He's Churchill with a fat cigar

And yet his fate seems signed and sealed
His horn is his Achilles heel

And as he charges, turns and brakes
The Chinese measure out his fate

Ingesting powdered rhino horn
To keep their old libidos warm

And turn the Durer back to stone
By picking up a mobile phone.

River Creatures

I am the heron
Praying for fish
On the plate of the moon
My twinkling dish

I am the stickleback of English streams
A silver comb
From a mermaid's dream

I am the pike
Who skulks alone
A cutlass
From a broken home

I am the Kingfisher
Soaring high
Oberon's jewel
In the Winter sky.

Stamp of Christ

The robin is nature's symbolic flame
Impervious to wind and rain
Transcendent on a frozen pail
The Stamp of Christ on Advent mail.

How the Robin Became

The dowdy bird at Christmas sings
A canticle on snowflake wings
For flying past the Magi's star
He found the cradled avatar
And sang a song on Mary's lawn
A Rubaiyat to greet the dawn

The rosehip bird at Easter brims
A chalice borne on angel's wings
For flying past The Saviour's cross
His breast was sprayed with scarlet drops
And now he sings on Easter morn
Respendent from a crown of thorns.

Rook

The rook
Has a black intelligence

An avian hell's angel
He loves his tribe

For he is the biker of the autumn skies

And he knows scarecrows
Are straw filled men

He skewers their eyes
To feed his friends

And lives aloft
In the rookery wood

In a nest of chapters
Oozing blood

And caws aloft
At the biker's hub

In a raucous querulous Hell Fire club.

A Land Rover's Valentine:
Discovered in the wanted columns of Auto Trader

Right...
I'm a
Sixteen valve
Four-wheel drive
Souped up
Diesel-powered
Transglobal
Off-road
Metal mercenary

HARD AS NAILS

Angry

(lonely)

Battered

(sad)

Looking for a small mini

.....To love.

Factory Farmed

The salmon farmer
Has impounded the constellations
Furled the sails of Magellan
Locked up the waterfalls
Switched off the moon
Turned the salmon's poetry
Into Gradgrind's fact filled prose
This battery farm of the water
Has sucked all the hazel wisdom from the Druid's fish
To give us his flesh on a Habitat dish
The call of the wild fills the salmon's soul
But the stars shine down on his festering shoal
A donkey of water he turns the wheel
Whilst the lice burrow into his pointless keel.

Salar

So weary after his long journey
Leaping the stairway
to heaven.

Salmon

Back full circle
The Old Man-of-War
Shows his keel
In his birthing pool

He has threaded the earth
Through the eye of his needle

Returned to spawn
By the Saxon steeple

And now he shudders in his shawl
of scars
Ebbing slowly under autumn
stars.

Queen of the Slipstream

Scenting her postcode
In water and stars
Leaping up to the letterbox bowl
The Queen of the Slipstream
Empties her hold
Franking her sailors
With stamps of gold.

Santa Claus Visits Earlham Road Cemetery, Norwich: For Jack and Robert Frost

The graveyard here is cold and bleak
But children here are born asleep
And I must leave them flowers of May
Before I wend my Christmas way

I give my harness bells three shakes
Then lift off through the drifting flakes
For I have many homes to seek
Where living children soundly sleep

And now the still born rest in peace
Beneath the winter's downy fleece
I've all those promises to keep
For all the Saviour's dreaming sheep

The world is lovely dark and deep
Above the lands where snowflakes sweep
But I have promises to keep
To all those angels sound asleep

And miles to go before I sleep
And myrrh to lay at Someone's feet.

Feeling sorry for the lonely scarecrow
I gave him a picture
Of Judy Garland.

On Good Friday
The rain lashed scarecrow
All alone.

Scarecrow

The scarecrow swings
In the rain drenched field
A creature made of roots and wheels
Who cannot think or hear or feel

And yet there's something in his stare
That makes me think there's someone there
A sentinel as pilgrims wend

A Janus as Four Seasons blend.

Easter Sunday
The scarecrow missing
From the moonlit field.

Magpie perched
On the scarecrow's shoulder
Caesar glinting in the
Autumn moonlight.

A Glass for Compo

Feeling sorry for the autumn scarecrow
I gave him the last
Of the summer wine.

Samuel Beckett's Scarecrow

Only me
Hanging around
Waiting for Godot...........

Searching for the answer to crop circles
Round and round
The scarecrow.

The scarecrow
Wearing her winter collection
Perspiring in the summer field.

Worzel Gummidge Gets Personal

Feeling sorry for the lonely scarecrow
I put an ad in the personals

Outdoor type
Would like to meet
Corn dolly
For bird watching

Must enjoy country pursuits

Field and Grid Reference supplied
(Previous Aunt Sallies need not apply)

No time wasters/football rattles or bin liners.

Tommy Cooper: Incognito

Feeling sorry for the sunburned scarecrow
I gave him a fez
Some clouded Raybans.

Scorpion

A question-mark
Above the sand

A shepherd's crook
A poison-gland

The sleek hull
Of a Trireme Queen

A Grecian floating war machine

And at the front a pair of claws
To feed the beast's revolving jaws.

S

Sea Anemone

I'm Cleopatra underwater
I'm Neptune's lissom
Rock-pool daughter

I flower with each incoming tide
The faithful moon keeps me alive

Provides my breakfast, lunch and tea
Served by the handmaid of the sea.

Sea Horse

A pregnant pause
In a sea of troubles

A glass-blown fern
In a stream of bubbles

A chessboard knight
On a looking-glass lawn

A mandolin prancing
To Neptune's horn.

Seals...?

Michelin mermaids
In tarpaulin slacks

Neptunian call-girls
Entrancingly fat

Sirens who slip
Between ocean and air

Then ooze onto beaches
To fuss with their hair

Divas who lurch
Between ocean and sand

Then cruise down to Cannes
To get cellulite tanned.

Shapeshifter:
A dream of Avebury after
viewing a painting at
The Sainsbury Centre Norwich

I walked beyond the painting's frame
To stand amongst the ancient stones
And felt The Iron Age stain my veins
Beside a tumulus of bones

The painted wind beat on my head
The air was filled with primal power
And as the sun sank in the West
A figure climbed a painted tower

He turned towards the setting sun
And then he raised a hawthorn wand
And as I watched he changed his song

The Druid blurred Became a swan.

January Storm

Timbers creaking
Far inland
Sirens in the winter rigging.

Skunk Chanel: For Ogden Nash

The skunk's so famous for his stink
Wild essence of a well blocked sink
His charming perfume made me think
Of bottling it for girls from Rome
Who'd spend long evenings on their own.

Skylark over Kitt's Coty

Dolmen doorway
Starchild path
Runic temple
Isle of glass
Mystic movement
Lie of land
Watch the skylark's spring ascension
Soaring from your dreaming hand.

Stonehenge Skylark

Dawn breathes the skylark
Through England's doorway
Blown from the lintel of spring.

Climbing Uffington vale
A skylark's bright alarum
Drifts across this empty hill.

I know this probably won't surprise you
But Bashlo the somnolent Buddhist sloth
Took ninety nine years to write a haiku...!

Sloth

I like to hang for hours and hours
And contemplate the lovely flowers
The world's much better when it's slow
And as the slowest I should know
There's too much rushing all around
There's too much volume.. too much sound
The jungle's filled with too much noise
There's hardly any equipoise
So if you want a tip from me
Just join the sloth fraternity
Then hang around for hours and hours
And contemplate the lovely flowers.

Snail Memory

On this earthen bank
A sweet shop of dew-glossed snails
Takes you back to childhood days
When your world was a sylvan cornfield
A feathered sea of golden waves.

John Clare's Candlemass

I woke to snowdrops being born
Like angels huddled on the lawn
And then I heard through coppiced thorn
The songthrush at The Gates of Dawn.

The Darkling Thrush:
By Jesus aged 4, Nazareth Elementary

This is the bird that Jesus made
Whilst playing in the second grade

From claggy earth
The darkling sky
A snatch of Mary's lullaby

The glad thing was
He made him wing
Across to Dorset
Carolling

The sad thing was
He made him sing
About the gladness God would bring

But left him by the coppice gate
Where Doubting Thomas lost his faith.

Dream Catcher

I spin my maze of silver air
From threads of Ariadne's hair
To catch etheric jewels that fly
Festoon them on my wheel of sky.

John Cooper Clarke's
Giant Squid Rap

Or Daphne entertains Priscylla and Charybdis
(A poem Tennyson might have written...
If he hadn't thought better of it..!)

I'm eighty feet from beak to sucker
Tea clippers are my bread and butter

At twenty thousand leagues I glide
With tentacles that suck and writhe

At twenty thousand leagues I hide
Then lash the sperm whale's oily side

My angler fish are chandeliers
That light my boudoir's nameless fears

And here I spread a feast for friends
Of Danish pastries filled with men

I am the kraken of the deep
The reason sailors seldom sleep

I'm eighty feet full fathom five
With dinner plates for Wedgwood eyes

At twenty thousand leagues I thrive
Godzilla's underwater bride

From twenty thousand leagues I rise
Medusa on the evening tide.

S

Grey Squirrel:
Earlham Road Cemetery, Norwich

The squirrel
Is sewing together the bones of the dead
A needle carrying the thread of spring
He is hop-skip-jumping past the tumbled graves
A silver surfer on an emerald sea
Cleaving his wake through the startled snowdrops.

Red Squirrel Memories

In Beatrix Potter's books
The watercolours fading
And out by Nutkin's isle
The tails no longer sailing.

I cup the leaf flame in my head
I hoard the haw light roaring red
And let it warm my autumn bed
Through winter storms I'm lantern led.

Red Squirrel

You glimpse him
As a hilltop on fire
Elizabeth's chestnut hair
A blink of burning memory

Cordite tinder box and musket

The Iron Age stain of hilltop towns
Now fading from our country's crown
The russet ink from Shakespeare's pen
That bound us as a race of men

You glimpse him
As the chestnut thread
That tied the May Pole round our heads

The broad-leaved woodland's natural heir
Who scampered round The Green Man's chair

But now the woodland's lost its light
The dryad has been put to flight

And where the jewel of Autumn flared
The Crown of England's dark and bare.

Sun Fish

Vast and round is the Sun Fish
A Salvador Dali kiss
Wobbling across the Pacific
Like a love-struck satellite dish.

Swallows

Electric blue tailors
In evening air
They are cutting the suit
That the sunset will wear
Flickering over a crushed-velvet sky
A squadron of scissors
Dog fighting flies.

Migrating Swallows

Sycamore seeds
Dipped in lapis lazuli

Mackerel who've gained their wings

Errant notes
From a summer chorus line

Coathangers
For the autumn
Wind.

Swallows Know

Swallows know when it's time to go
But people seldom do

(I thought there was going to be more to this poem
But swallows know when it's time to go
And poets seldom do).

Swans on the Wensum: Spring 1998

Gliding towards me
Five wild water snowdrops
Delicate glass-blown river lanterns.

Swans on the Wensum: Cow Tower Norwich Summer 1998

A flock of imperious table napkins
Demanding bread
And silver service.

Swans on the Wensum: Autumn 1998

Gently angel ships approached
A fleet of mist-wrapped ermine boats

Then through the mist I glimpsed three lights
A casement into paradise.

Swan on the Wensum: Winter 1998

In the evening's afterglow
Only when the swan glides
Can you separate snow from snow.

Swift

Summer's brightest adjective
The swift turns his blades
Into blue air
Flickers on earth's windshield
Then crosses the globe
Of your marvelling eye
An aerial cheetah
Oustripping a fly
A cadmium spark
In the gunpowder sky.

T

Winter Moon

Look up...
A flock of golden teal
Engraved on Wodin's frozen shield.

Going....Going...?

Where have all the tigers gone..?
Into the darkness every one.

And what will all the children miss..?
The burning of a fire like this.

The Blue Tit's Nest: For John Clare

Her nest is made when moss abounds
All gathered from the splashy ground
And fashioned like a wattle ruff
All daubed with lovely bits of fluff
A wicker grail for brindled eggs
On which she broods inside our shed
Then feeds them when their beaks break through
Like crocuses amongst the dew
The parents flying back and forth
From east and south and west and north
With nuts and seeds and twitchy grubs
All garnered with instinctive love
Until the day the fledglings fly
And leave this woven lullaby
And when they'd flown I peeped inside
And found this dead chick on its side.

The Irish Toucans

The toucans love the Irish brogue
And smoky pubs and panty hose

They really come here for the craic
These bright ceramic acrobats

They love to dodge the whirling flack
The hurling sound of ball on bat

For Dublin is their summer home
They nest in haunts where writers roamed

The drayman finds them flying round
The turrets of the morning town

They break open his bottle tops
And guzzle Guinness on the rocks

The broody birds of Trinity
They cohabit in groups of three

They sing the Rose of Old Tralee
Eat cockles, mussels by the sea

Then flock across a million garrets
As garrulous as Grimsby parrots.

If Yeats had seen the toucans fly
Across a starry crowded sky

He would have dumped the swans at Coole
Have broken every bardic rule

And written of the toucans' flight
Round Maud Gonne's comely bedside light.

Night Thoughts of an Oak Tree: For J.R.R. Tolkien

I am the sarsen stag
Tossing my antlers
In the wind washed forest.
I am Saint Francis
Preaching to The Parliament of Birds.
I am circles within circles
Each year is a ring
On my wooden fingers...
I am the clothes-horse
For all kinds of weather
An acorn thrown into the lake of time
I provide shade for my own enlightenment
In Winter
I am the pearly king
Covered as I am
In buds of starlight
In Summer
I wear the crown of the mistletoe vine
I am the oldest wood
In the oldest wood
Since my birth
I have sheltered Druids
Canterbury Pilgrims
And flower children
Kings have hidden in my gilded tines
Afraid only of adze and lightning
Ships, cathedrals
And the chain saw's whine
I take the long view
The years flicker by
My leaves take a sip
Of rainwater wine
I may put down roots here
I may put down roots
But let's not be hasty
All in good time
All in wood time..

Leatherback Turtle

She has been crying for millions of years

This beautiful pea-green boat
This upturned coracle of sadness

For millions of tears
Evolution has sucked her back

Out of the blue dress of the sea
And onto the sands of indignity

To lay the eggs that will in time
Reprise this mournful pantomime

As clockwork toys whirr out to sea
To start new turtle families.

Star Maker:
Tutankhamun's Lullaby

Each verse chanted on consecutive nights
by the priests of the chamber
before sealing the tomb

Night 1
Now sleep... for great Anubis
Who is death's right hand
Has steered your ship of heaven
Through our gates of sand
Then pray...for your mother who is blessed
Has pressed
The seed of great Osiris
In time's swaddling bands.

Night 2
Now dream...for creeping twilight
On the cooling sands
Has rowed the groom of heaven
Into moon-kissed lands
Then sing... for your father in the west
Has blessed
The fruit of mother Isis
With his timeless hand.

Night 3
Now wake...for great Osiris
Cooled by peacock fans
Has lit this spark of heaven
With a flaming brand
Then dance... for our Pharaoh who is lord
Has moored
The soul of Tutankhamun
In his starlit land.

U

Unicorns

A silver stallion's
Lance of light
Is flashing in the Arden night
And angels from the seven realms
Are greaved and metalled
Armed and helmed
They come with lovelight in their eyes
And on their unicorns they ride
A cavalcade of kings and queens
Across the fields of children's dreams.

Narwhals

Spiralling out of the Norse Eddas
Come the sea unicorns
Wave-maned horses of the Northern ocean
Grail Knights of the borealis
Blubbery Quixotes
Wielding their scrimshaw stalactites
Jousting on the margins of The Mappa Mundi.

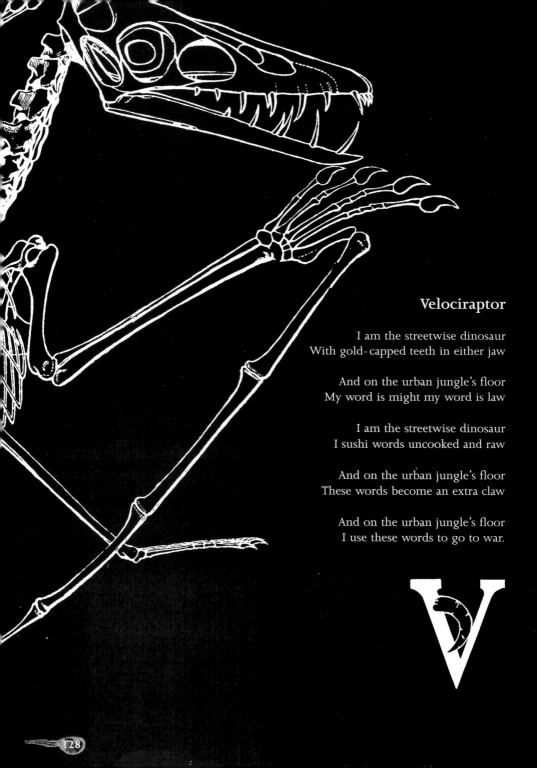

Velociraptor

I am the streetwise dinosaur
With gold-capped teeth in either jaw

And on the urban jungle's floor
My word is might my word is law

I am the streetwise dinosaur
I sushi words uncooked and raw

And on the urban jungle's floor
These words become an extra claw

And on the urban jungle's floor
I use these words to go to war.

Ratty: For Kenneth Grahame

The Wind in the Willows reveals the form
Of a water vole at The Gates of Dawn

On the banks of Toad's expansive hall
Where the ducks are a-dabbling up tails all

We find a hamper made of reeds
With potted shrimps and Stilton cheese

Comestibles of every kind
For a Cambridge Blue with a first-class mind

Upon a willow pattern plate
Beneath the weir below the lake

The water vole takes tea and cake
And reads the works of William Blake

He's English as the day is long
He hums the Cambridge Boating Song

And lies beside Old Father Thames
Through afternoons that never end

Just out of reach   Just round the bend
The Mole's enchanting whiskered friend.

Walrus:
In memory of
Barry White,
'The Walrus of Love'

Skinny-dipping can't describe
Balletic Bunters sunnyside
Three triple macs
A large french fries
Washed down with baked Alaska pies
Their teeth stick out like ice-pick forks
Encased in casks of Artic pork
Their eyes are red
Their hide is grey
They dine on clam-bake every day
They once inspired a fashion craze
For hirsute lips in byone days
Ungainly on the ice and snow
They revel in the seas below
A school of airships on the move
Dirigibles with flippered screws
They fly beneath the polar waves
Great Colonel Blimps at Fatboy raves
Astronauts of frigid space
Archangels of Titanic grace
Sumo wrestlers of the floes
The man, the bear, their only foes
Beneath the strobe light of the sun
The borealis leads them on
Great Barry Whites in Polar bars
They groove beneath the summer stars.

King of The Lewis Hoard

I sit in a chair
Carved from silence
Sensing the chequerboard of nights and waves
On which my sea lord's longship sways
Ferried in a box from The Golden Horn
Inlaid with the pearl of the unicorn
I am part of Tostig's precious navy
A Viking sea lord of the mind
Amongst the hold I bump and grind
With Freya here my precious queen
The Morningstar of Tostigs dreams
He saw a box from Samarkand
So loved the game he tried his hand
And had this chess set carved himself
Reflecting all his plundered wealth
We are the Gods of mortal men
The pantheon that succours them
Yet over there across the sea
Are other Gods that menace me
The chief of these is Christ the King
Whose bishops waiting in the wings
Are planning to ouflank my pawns
With promise of a life re-born
But whilst I sail the seven realms
With Thor and Loki at the helm
I will not fear his wooden cross
The raging fires of Ragnarok
I will not be baptized with water
For valour only comes with slaughter
Valhalla will assign my fate
The Fisherman may reach my gates
But then I will unleash my knights
My sea wolves of The Northern Lights
And in a brave and dreadful fight
Will slaughter all these Brides of Christ
Valhalla will assign my fate
Then Tostig say to Christ "Checkmate".

Note on poem. Long ago a
herdsman on the loch shore of
Lewis on The Outer Hebrides killed
a survivor from a shipwreck for the
bundle he was carrying. It
contained a heap of menacing little
carved images. Convinced that they
were the sailor's Gods, the
frightened killer buried them. Years
later he confessed when about to
be hanged for another murder, but
his prudent listeners decided to let
sleeping Gods lie. It was not until
1831 that a crofter rediscovered
them. When sent for sale they were
recognised as ancient chessmen
and are now acclaimed as one of
our greatest and most
enigmatic treasures.

The pieces exquisitely carved from
walrus ivory now reside in The
British Museum and in Edinburgh.
Chess has always been a battle
between opposing forces and in
this poem I line the Gods of the
Ancient Norse World against the
encroaching God of Christianity.
Christ of course was the victor for
in the end the Norse saw many
similarities between this
redemptive figure and their own
God Odin hanged on the
world tree. But the battle was long.

Folklore Myths and
Legends of Britain.

Weasel

A living stole with Rayban eyes
This Al Capone of svelte surprise
Slips furtively beneath the skies
His mind is full of thoughts of eggs
Of scrambled voles and otters' heads
And few elude this sylvan pro
Who guns for chicks in embryo.

The Ice Whale:
High Cup Nick, Yorkshire

Here lies the fossil
Of the ice whale

Here gapes the awesome baleen mouth
Which sieved and strained the mountain out

And here lie the rocks that pocked his skin

Embedded deeply
Driven in

He calved from valleys high up there
His mother polar wind and air

Then slithered down this millstone stair

A molten seething fissured thing
That scoured the land he floundered in

Then vanished in the harpoon sun
A hundred thousand spuming tons

That flowered like a million guns
Then let his life blood overrun

To leave this chasm
Rainbow-hung.

Windhover

The jump jet hangs
A solstice flare

The eye of Horus
Sights a hare
Who down below is unaware
The flail of Amun Ra is there

The jump jet hangs
Above the hare

Anubis reads the final prayer

The flail of Amun Ra is swung
A leveret enrobes the sun.

Our bonsai bird
The moonlit wren
This haiku flying from my pen.

Wren: For D.H. Lawrence

A tiny matchbox dinosaur
The hedgerow's
Chintzy minotaur
We view this thimbleful of bones
From safety
In our windowed homes
But if we'd met him
In the park
Before the sailing of the ark
He would be taller than the trees
And we'd be trying not to sneeze.

Wren for all Seasons

A thimble
Borne on autumn leaves

A snuffbox
Filled with summer seeds

Tom Thumb
Perched on springtime's palm

A haiku
For a winter psalm.

Xiphias Gladius

Errol Flynn
With added fins

Pinocchio
With water wings

A jousting knight
Beneath the foam

Neptune's barber
When in Rome.

Yellow Hammer

The bird that flies
Throughout the spring
With Colman's Mustard on his wings.

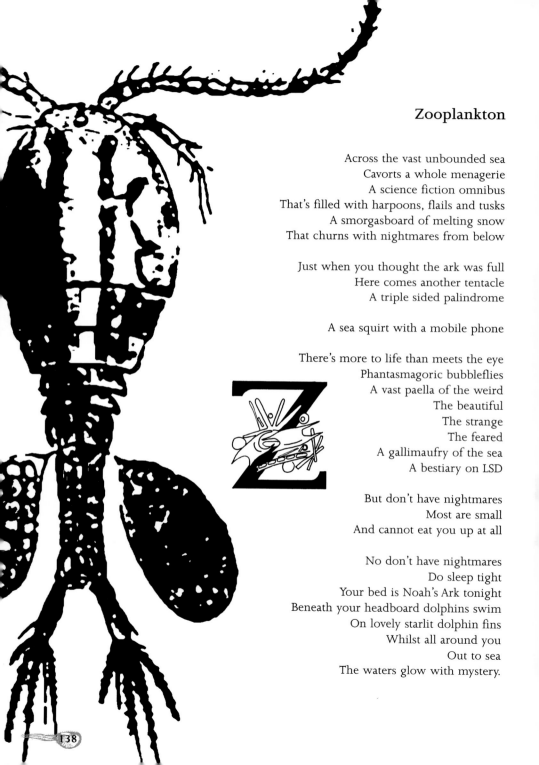

Zooplankton

Across the vast unbounded sea
Cavorts a whole menagerie
A science fiction omnibus
That's filled with harpoons, flails and tusks
A smorgasboard of melting snow
That churns with nightmares from below

Just when you thought the ark was full
Here comes another tentacle
A triple sided palindrome

A sea squirt with a mobile phone

There's more to life than meets the eye
Phantasmagoric bubbleflies
A vast paella of the weird
The beautiful
The strange
The feared
A gallimaufry of the sea
A bestiary on LSD

But don't have nightmares
Most are small
And cannot eat you up at all

No don't have nightmares
Do sleep tight
Your bed is Noah's Ark tonight
Beneath your headboard dolphins swim
On lovely starlit dolphin fins
Whilst all around you
Out to sea
The waters glow with mystery.

ONE IN MANY

I am the snake that sheds its skin
To let my soul light glow within

I am the butterfly of love
The Holy Ghost's eternal dove

I am the rainbow bird at dawn
Great Herne the Hunter's ghostly horn

I am the salmon and the seer
The spirit of the running deer

I am the Goddess and the sage
The flame that lights religion's page

I am The Buddha, Atman, Christ
Whichever path you feel is right

For I am everything you see
Creation is my wishing tree

And I am mountain, star and whale
The smile behind creation's veil.

"So we found the end of our journey

So we stood, alive in the river of light
Among the creatures of light, creatures of light".

Ted Hughes: *That Morning*

BTCV

Do you feel passionately about animals and the environment? Would you like to do something to help?

Since 1959, BTCV (formerly the British Trust for Conservation Volunteers) has been working with volunteers to protect and improve the urban and rural environment.

Today, we involve over 130,000 people from all walks of life, committed to the conservation of a vast array of habitats all across the UK, as well as in over 25 countries abroad. We operate through a network of around 150 local offices, so there is almost certainly something happening on your doorstep.

From planting trees and creating community gardens, to building otter holts and protecting butterfly habitats, BTCV gives you the opportunity to help your environment.

It doesn't matter how much time you have to spare – there's bound to be something to suit. And don't worry about experience either – BTCV provides all the training and support you need.

Most of all, it's a great way to make friends, have fun and look after the environment. So why not get involved? Here are just some of the ways you could join in:

- Come along to a conservation day – BTCV conservation days take place every week all over the UK.
- Go on a BTCV Conservation Holiday – from dry stone walling weekends in Derbyshire to two weeks' turtle monitoring in Thailand, these holidays offer an experience that last a lifetime. With prices starting from as little as £40, there's something to suit every budget.
- Join your local community or conservation group – BTCV supports a network of nearly 2,000 local groups, offering practical help and advice, grants and services including cost-effective insurance.
- Join a BTCV Green Gym – improve your health and the environment by coming along to these conservation sessions that have been shown to improve both mental and physical fitness. Make friends, have fun and get fitter – what could be better!
- Become a BTCV Volunteer Officer – hands on experience combined with training towards qualifications makes this a recognised programme throughout the environmental sector and a fantastic opportunity for anyone looking for a career in this area.
- Order trees, wildflowers, garden tools, practical handbooks and a whole range of other conservation-related products – visit www.btcv.org or call 01302 572244 for a free catalogue.

Whether or not you are able to give us your time, we also desperately need your financial support. Individual donations help pay for the training, clothes, tools and support needed by our volunteers without which they couldn't carry out their work to such great effect.

With your help, we can continue to inspire people all over the world to take positive and practical action to improve their local environment.

For more information about BTCV, our volunteering opportunities and how to make a donation:

Visit www.btcv.org
Tel: 01302 572244
Email: information@btcv.org.uk
BTCV, 163 Balby Road, Doncaster,
South Yorks DN4 0RH

BTCV in Leicestershire

From the National Forest to Leicester city centre, BTCV is active across Leicestershire and always on the lookout for more volunteers and supporters.

Whether you are interested in learning traditional country crafts such as dry stone walling and hedge laying, or you want to improve a scruffy patch of wasteland at the end of your road, we can offer support, advice and practical opportunities to look after your local area.

We run two regular weekly conservation groups, one based out of Leicester and the other from Coalville. From there, we go out and about across the county tackling projects as diverse as reed cutting at Narborough Bog to building otter holts alongside the River Mease. Newcomers are welcome – there's no charge and no experience is necessary – we provide the know-how, tools, safety instruction, transport and refreshment. Please join in!

We also work closely with community and conservation groups in Leicester, Loughborough, Coalville, Ashby, Ellistown, Markfield and elsewhere, helping local people to work together to improve the environment on their doorstep. From running community consultation days to health & safety training, we provide practical advice and support in all aspects of local conservation work. If you think we can help your group, or even if you just want tips on how to get a group started, please get in touch.

Finally, Leicester itself is one of the main bases for BTCV's pioneering Environments for All programme, providing specific opportunities for black, ethnic minority and disadvantaged groups to get involved in looking after their local area. This work is helping to show that the environment isn't just the preserve of the white, middle-classes but that anyone can get involved.

For more info on BTCV in Leicestershire, please contact:

BTCV
c/o The National Forest Company
Enterprise Glade, Bath Lane, Moira
Swadlincote
Derbyshire
DE12 6BD

Tel: 01283 229096
Email: Leicestershire@btcv.org.uk

BTCV in Norfolk

Volunteer opportunities

For 20 years BTCV has been providing opportunities for volunteers during weekdays, weekends and on Conservation Holidays in Norfolk.

We have centres in Norwich and Kings Lynn and our volunteers carry out practical work in a variety of interesting sites around the county in both rural and urban locations. Whatever your age, background or experience – we need you!

Heathland management at Mousehold Heath on the outskirts of Norwich, coppicing in Reffley Wood near King's Lynn, clearing scrub in the beautiful Norfolk Broads and erecting fences at Mile Cross are just some of the activities you could get involved in. Or why not learn how to make a willow wigwam or a wooden spoon on of our traditional craft training days?

Our project leaders provide all the training you need, while you can get out and enjoy practical activity, working in a group and discovering new places. It gives a great sense of achievement and you'll also find it a lot of fun!!

Community support

BTCV in Norfolk provides support for community groups who are involved in helping their local environment. The support includes help with housekeeping matters such as insurance, start up grants and information on project grants, as well as practical matters such as tools and project management.

Many local groups in Norfolk have received People's Places Awards that have helped to fund capital costs, training, insurance and on-going support so projects can be carried out to enhance local environments.

Training, education & work experience

From fundraising to hedge laying, why not give your skills a boost? BTCV Norfolk runs a programme of short, nationally certificated courses for all the community through the BTCV Institute of Environmental Conservation.

We also have full and part-time opportunities for Volunteer Officers, including leadership and project organisation experience, particularly relevant to those interested in a career in conservation.

For further information on BTCV's activities in Norfolk please contact;

Denver Slowther
BTCV Eastern Regional Office
Dragon Cottage, St Ann Lane
Norwich
NR1 1QG

Tel	**01603 767400**
Fax	**01603 767373**
Email	**D.Slowther@btcv.org.uk**

Life Size Seated Angel: Earlham Road Cemetery, Norwich

Photo by Richard Bonfield

THE POET

Richard Bonfield was born in Leicester on April 27th 1959 at 11.45pm: Taurus with Capricorn moon, Sagittarius rising and Scorpio mid-heaven. He shares his birthday with Cecil Day Lewis, Edward Gibbon, Samuel Morse and Sheenah Easton.

He moved to The Fine City of Norwich in 1977 to take an Honours Degree in Development Studies, then languished in 'The Graveyard of Ambition', 'Land of the Lotus Eaters' for the next two decades, pursuing a bohemian lifestyle as 'Jack of all Trades and Master of None.'

During a long and largely undistinguished career, he has variously been an advertising manager for *Cover* Norwich's equivalent of *Time Out*, a satirical columnist, a wholefood worker, a voluntary publicity officer for C.N.D, a bookshop worker, both commercially and for Oxfam, the assistant manager of an off - licence and a caterer.

He returned to the city of his birth four and a half years ago and is currently a member of the Beers Wines and Spirits team at ASDA Oadby, where he is "Always happy to help!"

His first self-published collection *A Bestiary an Animal Alphabet* was included in The Books of the Year in *The Independent on Sunday* in 1993 and his second collection *Swan for all Seasons* came out to equally favourable reviews in 1997.

Since 1989 he has had over 200 poems published in some 20 different magazines.

He was the Feature Poet for the summer issue of Poetry Nottingham International in 1999 and has won numerous prizes for his work, one of the most recent being his inclusion amongst the prize-winners in The *BBC Wildlife Magazine* Wildlife Poet of the Year competition in 2002 for the poem *Zooplankton* the penultimate poem in the present volume.

He is currently working on his fourth collection *A Scarecrow's Almanack* which takes you on a journey round the festivals of the original Celtic Wheel, and he is also deeply engrossed in a free-verse translation of *Beowulf*.

On his father's side he is descended from a Norman Lord and, on his mother's, reputedly from Robert the Bruce, which makes his full name Richard Norton Bonfield something of a Triumph..!

He is certainly not averse to Scottish Home Rule and has never suffered from Arachnaphobia..!

He is a committed vegetarian, a believer in The Perennial Philosophy and a dabbler in watercolours, ad-lib piano playing, countryside walking, fine wines and gourmet vegetarian cookery. His recipe for wensleydale, apricot and almond roast was a published prize winner in the ASDA favourites cookbook.

He is not, unfortunately available for weddings, or even the odd funeral, although he IS available for readings of both his poetry and The *Arthurian, Druid Animal Oracle* and *Greenwood Tarot*.

He can be contacted at

Coypu Publications

18 Poppy Close, The Maltings, Leicester LE2 6UR

Tel: 0116 2833727